tears of a lost soul

lashonder demery

S.H.E. PUBLISHING, LLC

Tears of a Lost Soul

Content Warning: This book contains themes of death, sexual abuse, and other emotionally distressing situations that may be sensitive to some readers. The content within is intended for mature audiences and may not be suitable for younger readers or those who are sensitive to such topics. Reader discretion is advised.

For information contact :
SHE PUBLISHING LLC | Munster, IN & Indianapolis, IN

Email: info@shepublishingllc.com
Website: www.shepublishingllc.com

Library of Congress Control Number: 2025933381
ISBN: 978-1-964061-26-9

Second Edition: March 2025

10 9 8 7 6 5 4 3 2 1

CONTENTS

FOREWORD

Since honoring the request of a friend, I accepted the role of Godfather for this brilliantly talented author, and I am so glad I did. Since then, I have witnessed almost every event of her life that is so courageously shared in this manuscript. From my point of view, I am truly convinced that God is faithful in restoring the lives of his children. It will become evident as you explore the pages of this book that Lashonder's life today is a testament to God's goodness and grace in the life of those who believe. This validates John 8:32 KJV in scripture, which says, "And you will know the truth, and the truth will set you free." It is clear for all to see that freedom is her reward. For the Lord has promised, according to Isaiah 61:3 KJV, "to appoint unto them that mourn in Zion, to give them beauty for ashes, the oil of joy for mourning, the garment of praise for the spirit of heaviness; that they might be called trees of righteousness, the planting of the Lord, that he might be glorified."

This autobiography displays all the trauma, dysfunctions, and devastation that seem to be commonplace in this generation today. Lashonder's resilience will encourage and uplift countless others traveling on similar journeys. This book is another tool of discipleship in the hand of God to bring about change in the lives of struggling victims who have fallen under the pressure of this evil world in which we live. *Tears of a Lost Soul* is filled with the transforming power of the Holy Spirit, and I believe that through this book, lives will be changed for the betterment and the building up of the Kingdom of God.

From a therapeutic perspective, this book can be a teaching resource for rehabilitation centers and recovery programs. Such a resource is used for teaching and encouraging clients on their journey to overcoming addictions and ensuring that a life of sobriety is indeed a possibility. This book is written from multiple perspectives. The author tells of the struggles she experienced firsthand, as she yields space for her children and grandchildren to express their accounts of how her addiction, incarceration, and the loss of her sons affected their lives. All these are powerful witnesses to clarify the struggles and pitfalls involved in the lives of those who encounter various types of addictions. This author's testimony of how she survived and lived to talk about it is a great tool to help others who are struggling to be victorious.

Reading this book opened my eyes to many truths about addiction and gave me a better perspective as a therapist. I invite you to explore the pages of this book, as I am sure you will be encouraged as well. May your life be empowered to conquer whatever journey you encounter while crying *"Tears of a Lost Soul."*

Grace and peace,
Gregory K. French

ENDORSEMENTS

My Dearest Lashonder,

I am so deeply grateful to have met you. As I listened to your story, overcoming so much pain, you took back your power, reclaimed your name and created a new version of yourself. Yesterday you were a victim, but today you are a survivor. You are truly remarkable, loving, blessed, worthy, and most of all, an amazing friend. I love you always and forever.

Dominique T. Jones

Hollywood script writers masterfully create motion pictures that take movie watchers on an emotional rollercoaster ride. Scene after scene, viewers watch intently to see the one slated to lose, rise to victory. When the moment of triumph manifests, the vigor is surrounded by a plethora of supporters. In some cases, even former naysayers are transformed into believers. In the end, the outcast is dubbed an overcomer, everyone cheers, and all is well. Someone said art is an imitation of life. For Ms. Lashonder Demery, real life experiences were the framework that created what the prophet Isaiah called BEAUTY FOR ASHES (Isaiah 61: 3) Lashonder is a certified artist who has taken broken pieces from her past and created a masterpiece that blesses the lives of many. Although she is still tapping into her many God- given talents and gifts, what she has discovered so far has broken generational curses and established a legacy for generations to come. She is a mighty woman of God whose faith is unshakable. She is a jewel who allowed trials of Life to chisel her into a fine precious gem. Her story is compelling. Her life has just begun. Hollywood has yet to tell a story like she has.

Tamika Starks

In Tears of a Lost Soul, Lashonder Demery has penned a powerful, heart-stirring message that resonates deeply with anyone seeking growth in their faith and deepening their relationship with God. With compassion and clarity, Lashonder guides the readers through her personal trauma, offering both inspiration and practical steps rooted in biblical truth. *Tears of a Lost Soul* is a beacon of hope and encouragement, reminding us of God's unfailing love and grace that is with us in every season of life. This book is a must read for anyone yearning to walk more closely with Yeshua and live out His purpose with renewed strength, joy and peace.

Your Sister in Christ,
Donna White

My Beloved Sissy,

First let me say I'm so very proud of you, the hurdles you've overcome and all the triumphs along the way. You are a true testament of an overcomer. We've had our share of ups and downs, but it's strengthened our bond over time and I'm grateful. This book is an explicit overview of your journey through life. Keep soaring high my Sissy for the sky is your limit.

Your Friend & Co-laborer in God's Kingdom
Minister Okerda Mitchell

PROLOGUE

I say this often, I am a "real" person with "real" problems. I have a past just like everybody else. I do not spend my time trying to cover up my mistakes and project this perfect person. I am not an entertainer. I do not thrive off of seeing people struggle, nor do I find room to judge and think more highly of myself than I should. In fact, writing this book was a humbling experience. It took every ounce of courage I had to do so. Today I stand on these words, and found them to be true (Revelation 12:11 (AMP) "And they overcame *and* conquered him because of the blood of the Lamb and because of the word of their testimony, for they did not love their life *and* renounce their faith even when faced with death"). I find my strength in Christ. He fights my battles for me. Through everything I went through, I wasn't sure if my life had purpose. I was no different than the fool that said in his heart, "There is no God". Everything I did, all of my actions, my lifestyle, decisions and beliefs spoke damnation over my life. It was my soul that cried out to a Living God who chose to save me. I did not save myself, and for that, I'm truly grateful. Let me be honest, I can't save anybody, but I can encourage and edify as many people as God put in my path. Maybe that person is you.

A couple of years back, when I decided to write this book, I had no idea my daughter, son and granddaughters would have testimonials for the book. At the time, my daughter wasn't speaking to me (she wasn't in my life), my granddaughters were 10 and 11 years old and my son was in prison. In other words, it wasn't in my plan, but God's plan. This is proof He will intervene into your life. My daughter shares her hardship of being abandoned by me. My granddaughters share the loss of their fathers (one to prison and the other to death) and my son shares the events leading up to murdering his brother.

We are inviting you on our journey. Just like us, you have a testimony!

MAY THIS BOOK BE A BLESSING TO YOUR SOUL!

TESTIMONIALS

MYCALS DIARY....

As a child I was not sure how to feel, nor did I understand how to process my emotions. I was moved around so much from one family to the next, it seemed as if I had a different family faster than I could adjust to the current one.

I had gotten accustomed to the fact that people did not stick around forever and would always leave. At least for me, this is what I saw, and how I felt being a young girl. However, I still feel this way at times during my adult years.

In my eyes, I had a mother who did not amount to anything for a long time. I thought to myself *"If she was not willing to be a parent to her own daughter, then who would."* My brothers were present for a short period of time, but eventually we were separated.

I felt an intense loneliness that is hard to describe unless experienced personally. I would stay up all night long to the point where my foster mother would call me a nightwalker. You would think once I found myself a little comfortable with my foster mother, I would be able to sleep, but this was far from the truth. I was afraid and humiliated.

Thoughts questioning *"How does a woman have children and not want them?"* would race over and over in my head. I would find myself not just thinking, but also saying the words "who in the hell does this?" But then I would think, '*I'm cool*', knowing this was not true.

Although I understood I was safe, this was not enough. Living in a lonely world, processing thoughts of a mother who was useless, led me to understand a mother was not needed.

For me, I never knew what the true definition of a mother was. This emotional heaviness I carried was a result of me being adopted at the age of nine or ten.

I was raised to be tough and survive in the world, but I still wanted and needed to be loved by my mom. I never knew what being loved by my real mother was or felt like until now. The way I would express my thoughts about my mother verbally was "if she had the strength to be a mother, then she should have done just that."

It was only natural for me to blame my biological mother for all these thoughts, feelings, and emotions. I just knew I was incapable of being loved by her or anyone else. So, I blamed the one person I knew that was responsible, my biological mother. Experiencing a relationship with her was not my thing. These feelings grew after I saw her less and less.

Growing up with my brothers in a foster home along with other foster children was a bit much for kids my age. Initially, I thought at least me and my brothers were no longer separated. However, I was still lonely, confused, and felt abandoned. This could have also been because I was the only girl until I begged for sisters. Even after this, I ended up with four, but they were in and out which was "pretty" strange.

Let me also mention it was weird having my last name changed while having to learn a new home. I was not going anywhere at the time. My brothers and I were there to stay. We did anything possible to make sure we stayed. As kids, we all wanted parents who loved us unconditionally. I do believe this was our case.

As time went by growing up, I started to develop resentment towards my biological mother. My father was around so I was not upset with him, nor did I hate him. He did as much as he could, so I respected him. For me, my mother was a different story. I did not like her and at the time, I barely knew what she looked like. While my father would try to say nice things about her, my foster mother would just be straight out honest.

She would say "Lashonder is sick and would get better eventually." But I wasn't dumb, and this was because of many of the things I remembered. I remember the many nights she did not come home. When she did return, she would be high and out of it. So, as I grew older, I started to forget about her and desired to not even think of her.

There were times when my foster mom would allow me to visit my blood family, but it was so touchy. She wanted me to know my background and allow me to decide how I wanted to handle these things. I visited for love, but the love connection was never present. The people I received love from (my foster parents), were not the ones I wanted it to come from. Love from them was not the same as what I desired to have from my biological mother, Lashonder.

So, by the time I was 16, my life was spiraling out of control. One of the things that hit me the hardest was my father passing away. I continued to enjoy being in a good home where nothing physically bad happened to me, but some decisions in my foster home did not seem fair. As I got older, Lashonder continued to try to reach out more, but I was not having it.

Of course, I did not care for her, why would I? She abandoned me to the point where I did not know who she was. On the last visit I had with her; she took the money my dad had given me and left in a car. It was hours before she returned. I was in the house alone until the next morning starving. My father came over and asked me where she was. I said, "She took my money and left." I explained to him that I had not seen her since. He gave me some more money plus the amount she took. My father called my foster parents to pick me up.

The next time I heard anything about Lashonder, I saw her in the newspaper one day when I arrived home from school. She had been arrested. My foster mother called me into the kitchen to show me the article. She had always explained to me that my mother's addiction was an illness. She never taught me to resent my biological mother. However, at a very young age, my emotions for her were stale. Of course, at this age I would see things differently due to resentment and abandonment.

Years later, Lashonder got out of jail and continued to reach out, but in my mind at the time, there was nothing she could say that I wanted to hear. What was the point of dealing with her for any reason? A scorned hurt is different when you start to become older. You might deflect your hurt on others without it being intentional, but it happens, and this is what happened in my case.

The neglect I experienced resulted in my thoughts being toxic and unhealthy. In my world, I thought of people being evil, so for me, I figured- *I might as well be evil too*. I viewed the world as a careless place and full of betrayal. I thought people in general were disappointments no matter what happened. Yes, I blamed Lashonder for this, because it all started with her. To me, she deserved most of the heat. My mindset grew to the point of hurting people as a form of satisfaction. My thought process was, I would get you before you got me. All these toxic things that happened tore me into pieces.

The saying that 'blood is thicker than water' was a lie to me. Resentment played a significant role in my life, along with other issues. I did not learn how to process this type of trauma until I became a little older. How cute is it to be 29 and continue to blame childhood trauma on everything but not including one's own adult decisions.

Through all the trauma, the true love I did experience came from a family that was not blood relatives. I learned what a family meant through them, but still, I did not understand love.

I had to learn how to allow myself to heal, let the unnecessary part go and view things from a "what really happened" perspective. This is when I learned to try and understand it from my mother's side of life and what made her make some of the decisions she made.

Yes, pain happens, but it is not meant to last forever, especially when you desire to receive your blessings. Life becomes the actions we put into it especially after experiencing pain, grief, loss and abandonment. It is possible to enjoy life while we are still here.

I am very grateful to be given another chance to know my biological mother. As I process this newness with her, I call her weird sometimes lol. However, I am still coming to know her, love her, and accept her for her. I also understand this is just as different for her because she never knew me as her daughter.

Today, we are learning each other and what it means to be a family. As part of this process, I had to realize, and accept she was dealt cards with many faces of trauma. So just like me, as a child, she was not sure how to feel nor did she understand how to process her emotions. As a young girl she would not have known how to handle the things that happened to her at such a young age.

She made decisions based on what was comfortable for her but also based on her not understanding.

Since I am a little older now, I have learned to just talk to her. She was a part of my healing journey because she was a part of the problems, I had that needed resolving. I needed my own answers, understanding and time with her. On my 29th birthday, I came to Houston after deciding to have lunch with her.

I explained to her that I needed her to help me battle issues that would continue to haunt me and our relationship. She was quickly willing to get on board with me during this journey. She listened and paid attention as I explained to her where I would like to be in life. Two weeks after this, I decided to move to Houston, and live with her. Her home was arranged as if I already lived there. 'Very awkward, very weird again' I thought, but in my head, this was something I had desired so I processed that things would be just fine.

Even though we have our different ways, things are going well for the time we spend together. We are also alike in many ways. I don't find interest in what she thinks or feels I should. I also understand she is still learning me, and I am still learning her. The experience of getting to know her as a mother at my age is also different and not easily explainable.

I don't call her Mom, and this is hard to break due to the past circumstances, but I also hope she does not find or see this as disrespectful. I can be honest and say she has some views I do not agree with, but I am still learning to know and understand her as well. We all have certain things about us that another person may not agree with. Nevertheless, she is still kind, smart, goofy and does not let her past dictate her future. She is a disciplined God-fearing woman and a go-getter, a major improvement to who she was before. Today I am proud of her; and the patience she has with me is amazing. I am very grateful to have her.

To those that have experienced this in their lifetime, it is ok to feel the emotions of resentment and abandonment but be sure to give yourself time to reflect on you. Everything takes time and nothing about it will be perfect. Be patient and seek out guidance. You must remember; for things to get better, you must initiate and stand through your process of change. Forgive yourself and those who have hurt you. Stay prayed up with God, believe in yourself and have faith. Miracles and blessings are real. You just have to take the leap!!!

FROM THE HEART AND BACK...

Hello, my name is Aaliyah Williams. I am 12 years old, and currently in the 7th grade. I will explain how a tragedy in my life affected and changed me, how it made me feel when it happened and how I currently feel today. I will share the lesson I learned from it, and how it made me a better and stronger person. Then I will reveal my understanding of what happened inside of me.

I was only 9 years old in the 3rd grade when I found out my uncle passed. The shocking part is, my daddy was the reason for this tragedy. I remember it like it was yesterday. It was testing week in school, Monday, April 19, 2019. I remember coming home from school feeling tired and quickly falling asleep. As I woke up later that same day, my siblings were asleep, but my mother was awake. I didn't know what time it was at the moment, but I remember going up the stairs and using the bathroom. My mother told me to do something I can't recall, and I did. She called my name again, but this time it didn't sound right. I went and stood in front of her; It was like I knew she was going to tell me something bad, and then she said it, "your daddy killed Trent." I burst out crying, I couldn't help it. We began preparing to leave our home to go to our papa's house, who already knew about what happened because of the news report. So, I got in the car with my sisters, who were 5 and 7 years old at the time. I broke the news to them as best I could, but they thought I was playing. I told them again in a way they would understand I was not playing. They soon broke out crying. Finding that out was a life-changing moment for us all.

For the next two days, we stayed at my papa's house. I didn't go to school or anything. In my 9-year-old mind, I wasn't crying because my dad was going to jail, I was crying because my uncle was gone and wasn't coming back. I felt like it wasn't time for him to leave, but everything happens for a reason, at least this is what I still tell myself daily. I ask myself all the time, *'Am I sad about my daddy being in jail?'* To tell the truth, I'm not, but that's just how I feel. Nobody can change how I feel about him being in jail. It's not that I'm mad about the situation, because I'm not. I'm disappointed. One can see what wrong decisions, drugs and an unstable state of mind can do to you in the long run.

It really didn't feel real for a moment, but just look at this, who in the world would want to tell someone, "My daddy is in jail, because he killed his twin brother"? I'm pretty sure no one would want to say that. I hate the fact that my dad did that to Trent. It doesn't feel good to know my dad did that to my cousin's dad at all. It's something I wish didn't happen.

This is how I feel about everything now. I feel like it wasn't time for my uncle to leave. It's like I don't care to talk to my daddy. Why? I really don't know. When I do talk to him, it just doesn't feel right. It's like everything is off. Then those questions come to my head after I have a conversation with him, *"What was he thinking when all that happened? "Why did it have to go down like that?" "Why to Trent though?"* I try my best to have a good relationship with Trent's oldest daughter, my cousin, because of the way things went down between our dads. I feel like Trent didn't deserve to leave so early. My cousins don't deserve their father to be gone because of my daddy. This is not right. In my mind, it's never going to be right. Let me say this, nobody deserves to lose their dad over some stupid unnecessary thing, but it happened and there isn't anything I or anybody else can do to change it.

The Lesson I Learned...

Don't do drugs! Spend as much time with the people you love because you never know when they will be gone. Only God knows. Use your mind with the best knowledge you know, to do the things to keep you in your right mind. Don't let stupid things break, mess up or ruin your relationship with your loved ones, family.

My understanding of what happened. Some might say my dad made a mistake because of the drugs, and him not being in his right mind. None of that matters to me. At the end of the day, he still did it, and that wasn't right. It's never going to be right. Trent didn't deserve that, and my dad should've known better. Like who would expect their dad to kill their uncle (his twin brother) just like that? Then the way he did it was crazy. The questions played over and over in my head. *'Did you not stop and think about what you were about to do? Did you not think about what was going to happen to him? Did you think about how that was going to make everyone else feel?'* It doesn't seem like it. It seems like he knew what he was doing, and that's sad, and not right at all. I wish one day my daddy would have enough brain, or you can say enough knowledge to get in his right mind and say that he is sorry to the people he hurt, but instead, he talks like it was the right thing to do. I know that he was wrong. I want to hear him say it. I want him to know he was wrong, not because everyone else says he was wrong. He needs to know he was wrong, and not act like the person he was when everything happened. He needs to be real with himself. If he can't admit he was wrong, and mean it with his heart to his kids, Trent's kids, my granny and everyone else, something is seriously wrong with him. The way everything happened, he must be one crazy person to think his kids and everybody wants to talk to him. I'm 12 years old, and I'm smart enough to know that what he did will always be wrong.

I just know that the whole situation broke my granny. She was getting herself together, and one of her sons went wrong. This tragedy will always and forever hurt his loved ones; It doesn't matter if they don't cry about how much they miss him; everyone is still hurt about his death.

I'm going to stay strong for my granny. I don't like crying in front of her about Trent's death. If God got my granny, God got me. I'm going to be somebody big in my life, and I'm going to make sure of this. People might make mistakes, but learn from your mistakes; don't repeat them, or act like they are ok, when they aren't.

A TRAGEDY THAT CHANGED IT ALL...

Hi, my name is Taliya Taylor; I am 12 years old and currently in the seventh grade. I would like to explain how a tragedy in my life affected me. What I experienced changed something in me that would impact me for the rest of my life. Here, I explain how I felt at the time and how I feel today. Experiencing this type of trauma made me a stronger person and gave me a different perspective on life.

First of all, I was definitely "a daddy's girl". So often, I would wonder why my father was not around as often as he should have been. Even though I did have some understanding, he was constantly caught drugs, guns, and violence. I still considered him a great dad and we had our own moments, but this did not change my perspective of him.

He was in and out of the system, but April 19, 2019, changed this. My father and his brother argued quite a bit. On this day, the argument resulted in my uncle shooting and running over my father several times.

When my mother arrived and walked into my grandmother's home, which is where we were at the time, her exact words were "Your uncle Trevor killed your father." I responded with "Mama you are playing." I immediately burst into tears once mama gave me that look. She was not playing.

I feel like Trevor should have known he was wrong, whether drugs were involved or not. I felt that he should have thought about his actions, his decisions and how the family would be impacted. Currently, Trevor is sentenced to life and fifty years in prison. My thought process is not, *"Oh he is getting what he deserves."* This is because he is someone's father too.

I remember this being some sort of breaking point for me because I did not get the chance to say goodbye. Three years after this, my twin cousin and I were separated. Our parents did this because they figured it was best. We did not communicate as much after she moved, but we also did not know how.

We were so overwhelmed at the fact that we were not going to see each other as much. We were used to seeing each other every weekend with all the cousins, mostly being together. We had to accept the decision that this was *actually* happening to us. This separation was also part of my reason for acting out at the time.

As time passed, we were able to spend time with each other again. Today, I am grateful that we still have a relationship, and we are closer than ever before. The tragedy and our understanding of each other is one of the reasons we are close. We currently have a bond that no one can break. She was the only person I felt like understood me emotionally and mentally at the time we experienced our tragedy.

Eventually over time, I corrected my negative behaviors. However, I have not fully accepted that my father is gone and not coming back. Honestly, I have delusions of my father that he is still present. Going through this hardship has continued to be difficult at times for myself and other family members. My mother for one, because even she has not fully accepted that my father is gone.

This was a tragedy I would not want any family to experience. Because I still have love for Trevor, I was able to forgive him. Even though this is the case, this is not something one ever forgets. I don't want individuals to only see my uncle killing his brother. I want people to also see healing is always possible. I learned to always think about my actions and never make a decision that could damage someone mentally or physically.

LIKE MOTHER LIKE SON...

My name is Trevor Williams. I am one of Lashonder's twins, the oldest son. I was born September 6, 1990, and during that time my mother was selling and using crack cocaine. In the midst of her being in the streets, and all that came with it, I was thrown into foster care, me, my twin and my sister.

When I was in foster care, my siblings and I bounced around different foster homes until we were comfortably adopted. While this was going on, my mom was still drugging and into the street life heavy, but she always kept trying to get us back. By her committing crimes of different kinds to support her crack addiction, the state wouldn't let us go back while she was in this condition. We all stayed in contact with her, and she would come visit us every chance she could.

While in foster care, all my mama's children were adopted by the same couple. They had a son. I was adopted when I was in the fifth grade. My adopted parents did more for their biological son than me and my siblings. Because of this, it led me to become rebellious and jump into the streets. I looked for the love that I was missing from my mother and didn't get it from my adopted parents, so I looked towards the streets for it. This led me to experience a lot of traumas, which ultimately led me to start following my mom's footsteps. I was into the street life heavy, selling drugs, robbing, killing and toting a gun everywhere I went. I was trying to fill that void that was in my heart with the lifestyle of the streets.

During this time of my life, my momma was in prison. She changed her life while she was there, but I was getting deeper and deeper into the street life. She, however, put God first. In April of 2017, my mom was released from prison. She let God direct her life and told me I needed to get out of the streets. She always stayed on me about changing my life.

The same year of her release, I went to jail (2017-2018). Upon my release, my twin brother told me he was an informant for the Shreveport Police Department. This opened a new can of worms and destroyed our trust. Soon after that, I jumped back into the streets, because that's all I knew. I started selling and using methamphetamines. My twin and I started getting high together. One time, he turned on me with the police and threatened to kill me. The outcome of that was, I killed him. So now, I am in Angola (Louisiana State Penitentiary) serving a life sentence for second degree murder. All this could have been avoided if I had listened to my momma and put God first like she told me.

Presently, I have found God. My mom and I have been praying together. I have seen the change my momma has gone through, and that same change has now taken effect on me. We communicate daily and talk about the bible, and she is my spiritual advisor as well. I love my momma with all my heart. She is my inspiration and motivation. I don't know what I would do without her.

God blessed me with a beautiful momma, and He has shown me what He can do for me when He shook my momma back. Now God has touched me with that very same miracle. Like mother like son, we both follow the same Father, God the Almighty.

TO MY DECEASED SON
"STILL IN MY HEART"

TRENTON WILLIAMS

 On my worst days I thought of you. Even when I was lost and confused, you were always in my heart. For the times I tried to get my life together and failed, I never thought in a million years once I did you would be gone. As a child, you had strong determination. I remember you not being afraid of anything or anyone. You were so brave.

Much of your life passed me by because of my addiction. But I do remember several encounters with you, and I could see you were angrier at me than your twin brother. You found it more difficult to forgive and embrace me than he did. I understood that. I was harder on myself than you were.

I realize that I didn't give you the life you deserved, and I still believe if I had gotten sober sooner, you would still be here. It breaks my heart that I couldn't save your life and share the life I now live with you. Rest in peace my dear son. I miss you and I love you dearly.

THE BIRTH OF IT ALL

"*Tears of A Lost Soul*" is based on a true story. It will inspire some and captivate others. The intended purpose of this book is to encourage you to rise from the ashes, finish what you started, take what could have destroyed you and make it your miracle, to bring families together through their struggles and promote healing. The author describes how her childhood trauma, substance use, toxic relationships, mental health issues and multiple forms of abuse caused her to lose her mind. She lost herself, her soul and her children. She gave up her will to live, and shame became her master. In this book, you will see how she was rescued from a road that was leading her on a path to destruction. Her life has been redeemed, and she wants to share her story with you.

My prayer is that this book will reach women, men and children who have been violated one way or the other through drugs, rape, domestic violence, molestation, sex trafficking, abandonment issues or adoption.

This is the revelation of "Tears of A Lost Soul."

CHAPTER 1:
LIFE SIGNIFIES HOPE

A baby girl was born November 21, 1972, to Valerie Denise Demery and Herbert Lee Dotson. At the time of pregnancy, my mom was 12 and my dad was 17. She gave birth to me at the tender age of 13. Of course, she was young, her first year of being a teenager, and in my opinion, this alone is a major hardship for any child this age. Plus, my mom almost lost her life-giving birth to me. She had to undergo major surgery to save her life or mine. One of us was not supposed to make it, but we both did. After this incident, which is marked as the first tragedy of our life, the story begins.

My mom and I were first raised by my grandmother, Lessie B. Demery and then by my great-grandmother, Arvesta Anderson. After my mom recovered from giving birth to me, she continued middle school and went on to Green Oaks High, graduating with honors. I started in Daycare at the age of 5 and kindergarten the following year.

Up until my 5th-grade year, I lived with my grandmother. I was an honor roll student at Northside Elementary from first through fifth grade and started my cheerleading experience in the third grade.

In my early years, I recognized my grandma as my mom; and even at that time, I noticed I was missing my mom. I knew my mom was there, but we didn't spend a lot of time together. She was in high school. I remember her being in the band, singing in talent shows and winning!! She graduated as valedictorian of her class despite her setback. Shortly after that, she moved away from home to stay with her boyfriend. Things changed and I realized I was seeing my mom less and less. In the times I did see her, she would tell me that I would come live with her soon. Over time, this promise came true.

CHAPTER 2:
A PROMISE CAME TRUE

One day, she came to pick me up and told me to pack my things. That day my life transitioned into new surroundings. I was in a new home with my mother and her boyfriend, which was completely different. I was no longer sheltered, nor did I receive the parental guidance my grandmother gave me. The home was more spacious and beautiful, but I had more rules. I remember being so excited about settling into my new home. Yes, I had my own room, and this brought me great joy!! I learned many responsibilities such as chores, scheduling my day and keeping appointments. I did not have to worry about these things as much when I lived with my grandmother. I was her baby, and she treated me like a baby. I may have washed dishes when I lived with her, but nothing major. I was not cleaning, cooking or washing clothes. My granny did everything for me, and she often told me we would run away together. As I said, my new home was beautiful to the eye and disciplined for the touch, but let's see what happens next.

CHAPTER 3:
UP TO NO GOOD

At the age of 11, I was accepted into Caddo Middle Magnet. Our 5th-grade class from my elementary school was chosen to test for this opportunity. However, I had my sights set on Linear Middle School (the neighborhood school), which was right down the street from where we lived. All my peers were going there, and of course, I wanted to go to the middle school we all heard about while in elementary.

By the time summer was over and school was getting ready to begin, my mom had made up her mind, I was "definitely" going to the magnet school. I attended, but did not want to and my academic performance was not as good as usual. I am sure this was due to me not wanting to go there in the first place. Nevertheless, I did pretty good, but for some reason, I was always afraid to fail. I worked hard, but not hard enough. We all know what this means, I was just getting by.

At the end of each semester, I would ask my mom if I could go to Linear. Sometimes she would say no, other times she would say let her think about it, and a few times she would say it's up to me. So, we played the cat and mouse game about this decision, as going to Linear the following year would fall in my favor.

My mom said, "You should ask yourself why you want to go to Linear." In my private thoughts I was contemplating, I could experience middle school like I heard about it. I wanted to run with my neighborhood friends, be fast, have a few fights, find a boyfriend and see who was smoking weed. At this time, I was already smoking weed from time to time, and my mom sold it.

'How easy would it be to steal a little, take it to school, sell some and share it too?' I thought. What other way to become popular, plus I was cute. Not to mention my mom sold clothes. Her boyfriend was a truck driver for major clothing stores around the area. He would bring boxes of name brand clothes, shoes and tennis home to the point where we had a store full. I was dressed to impress, smart in school and an only child. So of course, I was spoiled, looking through the eyes of a teenager and thought life was just fine.

At the age of 15, my mom taught me how to drive and later gave me a car. She bought it for me to attend my summer job at a local college. I didn't have a license, but I would drive to work each day. The university was in our neighborhood, not far away. My first job was an exciting time for me. In those days, smoking weed was popular for the people in my circle, family and community. I was an honor student in high school, on the varsity cheerleading team serving well and doing well, yet smoking marijuana. I would smoke before school, church and choir practice. So, getting high was normal. I did not know at the time that my behavior was bazaar, and my decisions were havoc. I exemplified addictive personality disorder in my early years long before my habit worsened.

CHAPTER 4:
BEING LEFT ALONE

A few other things happened during this era. My mom's boyfriend allowed his son to move into the home. Everybody under our roof started drinking and drugging. Not only that, I noticed the son and the father had their eyes on me. Before either one of them touched me, I knew they liked me in the wrong way. The fears I had because of this unstable environment grew stronger so I began smoking marijuana more. The discipline that was once in the home was no longer there. During this time, I began to feel unsafe staying with my mom.

I can't remember why, but my mom decided to go get a job. She was still selling marijuana and clothes but ended up working night shifts at a juvenile home. This didn't last very long. She was using and selling illegal substances on the job and finally resigned because they accused her of it.

During that time, I had a few encounters on separate occasions with the father and son. Neither one of them knew that the other one was trying to sleep with me. They both would choose a time when the other one was not looking or gone. The son had a different approach than the father. He filled my head with promises as a friend to gain my trust. The father would walk in the kitchen the nights I was washing dishes, touch my backside and walk away.

I fell into sexual advances with the son, and one night the father caught us. He did not say one word. He closed the door and kept quiet. He held the information until he was ready to tell my mom, and eventually he did.

CHAPTER 5:
FIRST HEARTBREAK

Over the next couple of years as a teenager, a lot happened. I lost my virginity, my addiction progressed, and my mom started using crack cocaine again. I never knew she smoked it in the past, until one night she explained to me that she had kicked the habit before, and she could kick it again. She was not working anymore, only selling clothes, crack cocaine and weed.

All of this got out of hand, and it grew even worse when the boyfriend lost his job. The house became a house of hustle. People were coming in and out, smoking, sometimes staying for days at a time. In my opinion, everything became unglued at its worst when the boyfriend started smoking crack too. Shortly after that, I was tired of the sexual interactions with the son, the inappropriate touching by the father and so I told my mom. At this point, in anger, the father told my mom about him catching me and the son having sex. To add to this injury, my mom packed me up, put me out and took me to my great grandma's house. She told her it would be better if I stayed at her house. My mom stayed with the boyfriend and matters got worse.

A year or so after this episode, I started smoking crack and dropped out of school after receiving an academic award scholarship. I was one semester away from graduating and this was a major turning point in my life. I was heartbroken from being separated from my mom and even more hurt that she stayed with the boyfriend.

Dropping out of school became a disaster, a living hell. The little structure I had was gone.

CHAPTER 6:
HIGH SPEED CHASE

Times were rough, and supporting my habit wasn't easy. I didn't know much about hustling, but my mom and the people I knew did. I would lean on her or them to support my addiction. In the beginning, I depended on her to find men whom I could sleep with for money, but eventually I didn't need her for that anymore. There were others who shoplifted and sold goods to make ends meet. It was just a dog-eat-dog world.

Out of the blue one day, one of my childhood friends asked me if I could borrow my mom's car to take her shoplifting. She explained she could get $100 dollars for ten newborn-baby outfits. She went on to say she would split the money with me and my mom. I asked my mom, and she said yes. We got into the car and headed out. She asked me to take her to Family Dollar, and stated she would make it quick. When I pulled into the parking lot, a few people were walking toward the Family Dollar. It was in a shopping center on North Market close to our neighborhood, so we were familiar with the area. As I slowed down to let her out, we noticed an elderly lady making her way toward our vehicle to cross the walkway to enter the shopping center. My friend said to me, "Slow down!" As I slowed down, she opened the door and snatched the elderly lady's purse. In shock, I drove off when she slammed the door shut, not knowing some part of the lady's dress was caught in the door. I drug her appropriately 21ft before her body went limp. I even remember the smell of her skin against the pavement. I hurried out of the parking lot, hitting one cement pole and one car.

After exiting the parking lot, I drove at a high-speed, running lights in fear of what had happened. Maybe five minutes into the drive, in my rear-view mirror I saw flashing lights. I could also hear sirens. The police were after us. I managed to stay far ahead of them as I made it back to my mom's house. We jumped out of the car and ran into the house. My mom asked what happened. We explained we snatched a purse, and she asked us what was in it. We didn't know. We never got a chance to look. She opened the purse to discover $12 dollars. We all looked at each other in regret. Minutes later, the sound of the sirens drew closer. The police were outside surrounding the house and commanding us to come out. My mom asked who snatched the purse. I looked at my childhood friend and said, "She did." My mom looked at her and said, "Well you go out." She went out the door and surrendered herself. They asked about the driver. At the time, she didn't say a word, but eventually she told them who I was.

CHAPTER 7:
CAPTURED BY MISTAKE

This was my first time on the run or in trouble with the law. Some days I was afraid, and other days I was not. I guess it was contingent upon whether I was high or not. I knew I wasn't going to turn myself in, although I needed to. I had no place to hide, nor did I know how to. Sadly, I ran out of places to go.

One day, as I was walking, a couple of guys driving a Ford truck stopped to pick me up. After getting inside the vehicle, they offered me a ride home, some money and a drink of alcohol. One of them stated they wanted nothing in return, only to get me home safely. I didn't believe that, but maybe it was true. I was very skeptical considering my circumstances, not theirs. I had been through so much at this point, I didn't trust them. Reluctantly, I took a drink and minutes later, I was passed out.

I woke up with no clothes sitting between the two men. As I was collecting myself, I gathered my surroundings. All I saw was woods. I asked where we were and the one to my right punched me in my jaw and told me not to say a mumbling word. I was terrified at this point and my anxiety intensified as I was shaking like a leaf. I listened quietly as they made plans to get rid of me. They had no intention of letting me live.

As we sat there, another car pulled up on the side of the truck. The driver stepped out, walked up to the truck and told them he was ready. He asked them where my clothes were. They said, "She doesn't need them, throw this jacket around her." I exited the truck, got into the back seat of the car and we drove away.

We were going down a dark dirt road with woods on each side. I was going to jump out the car, but I just didn't know when. In my mind, I would wait until I see a house or porch light. The car wasn't going fast, but not slow either. I would guesstimate about 25 mph. I began to feel strongly that my chance to exit was approaching. I then saw a double wide trailer with a porch light. A tall, wired fence was around it and a Doberman Pinscher dog was inside the yard. This was my chance. In fear, I grabbed the door latch, jumped out of the car, ran to the fence, and leaped over it. The car heightened its speed and kept going. The dog was constantly barking at me. I yelled a few times until someone came to the door. A Caucasian lady opened the door and shouted back into the trailer that a naked woman was in the yard. A Caucasian man came out and grabbed the dog. The lady brought out a blanket and walked me into the house.

They proceeded to ask me what happened, and I told them. The man assured me I was in good hands, and he was a sheriff. I learned I was in Longview Texas. They would have to escort me to the state line in order for me to get back to Louisiana.

Unless I had a relative to come get me, I would be transported by authorities, and they were looking for me to arrest me.

The sheriff asked me if I wanted to make a call to my relatives or wait for the police. I called my great grandmother and told her what happened. She asked me to hand the phone to the person who let me use the phone. She told the sheriff I was on the run and to make sure I didn't get out of his sight. She told him to bring me to the state-line and let the authorities handle it from there.

CHAPTER 8:
BITTER SWEET

My first ride to jail as a juvenile, I remember being mad at my great grandmother, thinking to myself *she turned on me*. At the same time, I was drowning in relief. This was my rescue. I was still alive. I nearly lost my life. As I rode in the back of the police car in handcuffs, I cried. I was headed to jail wrapped in a blanket feeling "big" sorry for myself. I didn't know what would happen next, but yet I felt safe. I had not felt this safe in a long time.

When I got there, I was booked in and given a uniform. The officer on duty took me to the back and the first person I saw was the girl that I had committed my crime with. We spoke and she asked how they caught me. I told her about the entire story later, but not at first when she asked. I knew she had given them my name and I really didn't want to talk to her. The investigator I spoke with prior to me being booked in said a few things to confirm my fall partner did not have any problems giving them my name. I didn't have time to be mad about that, yet I was reserved. On another note, I was just happy that I made it through that night.

As I walked into the day room, someone said, "Your grandma is here!" My grandmother was a cook at the juvenile center. This made me happy, yet sad, because I knew I had to face her. They fed us through a window, and maybe an hour after I got there, it was feed-time. When my grandmother opened the window to serve, she called my name. I walked over and we both began to cry. Another cook came to complete serving the feed-up and allowed me and my grandmother to have our moment.

I was a size 1 and she hadn't seen me in a while. As she cried, she said, "You're so small" and somehow that made us laugh through our tears. I didn't eat that day. I was there a week before I could eat, but when I started eating, I gained some weight. As the months went by, seeing each other got easier and the burden of the arrest and what I had done got lighter.

The year of 1989, I was sentenced to juvenile life for purse snatching. The victim passed after we were sentenced. The sad part is, I never got the chance to say I was sorry. I was to serve at the JRDC facility until I was 21.

Due to good behavior, I ended up doing 18 months.; I was released to a girls' home sooner than I expected.

CHAPTER 9:
DOWN SOUTH

In March of 1990, I was released from JRDC to a group home called the Rutherford House. Looking back at the conditions of JRCD, I was glad to leave there. The cells were unusually small, and they fed us through a flap. We walked to the kitchen once a day and the food was horrible. Often, it tasted old, and they served it cold most of the time. They worked us in a field from 5 am to 3pm. We were given gardening tools to till the ground, and the lawnmowers were non-electric. The place was small and usually packed with females from New Orleans and Shreveport. None of us got along. I considered this a hard time, I never made commissary. I didn't get a visit during this time, or an opportunity to communicate with my family at all. I wrote letters, but no one wrote me back. I often wrote to ministries, and they would respond from time to time.

One time I got into a fight. They locked me down, tied my feet together and my hands behind my back. They laid me on my belly and left me in a cell for 48 hours. I promised God if He ever got me out of this one, I would never do anything wrong again. After that situation, I never got into another altercation. Six months later, I received the good news that I was going to a group home close to where I live. And surely, I was excited about that.

CHAPTER 10:
BACK TO THE CITY

I didn't mention this before, but the childhood friend I was arrested with was shipped to JRDC with me. When I left to go to the group home, she was transported there with me as well. So, we ended up at the same place throughout our incarceration. We were also released around the same time. I had known her since we were 10 years old; as we got older, we got high together, hung out and as you can see, got into trouble. At the age of 43, she died of an overdose.

During my stay at the group home, a few good things transpired. I was introduced to individual/family counseling, I attended peer support groups and was granted access to going home on weekends.

Speaking with the counselors was not easy. They asked me to share personal things about myself I was not ready to disclose. On top of that, neither my mom nor my family ever showed up for the family group. I found out on one of my weekend passes that my mom was still getting high.

So, despite all that had happened to me, I was still returning to an unhealthy environment. This does not excuse my mentality, but it didn't help either. In other words, I was thinking about getting high again before I did it. The main three rules were no sex, no drugs and come in by curfew. Throughout the week, we were to attend all groups and go to school. I started off breaking the weekend rules by having sex and next thing you know, I was pregnant. This happened two months before I was released from the group home, and they never knew.

CHAPTER 11:
LOST AND CONFUSED

In May of 1990, I was released from the group home. I came home to my great grandmother pregnant, but I didn't tell her until I began to show. She pretty much figured it out. I was 18 years old recovering from a juvenile life sentence and the things I had done in my past. I was an emotional wreck and did not know how to seek out answers on my own. I didn't know how to ask for help, where to get help, or why anybody would help me? I was in a bad place and didn't know how to get out.

I was happy to be out of jail, but where should I go from there, was the question. I was pregnant with no job and living with my great-grandmother. She was my Madea. She didn't have a lot. She made do and loved us with all she had. She always provided a family home, but we didn't have much. My family was poor, and we lived in a lower-class neighborhood. There weren't many options available that I knew about, nor did I have the emotional or mental support that I needed.

I managed to stay sober during my pregnancy. At my fifth checkup, I learned I was having twins, my babies would come prematurely, and one of them was breech, meaning one of them was turned the wrong way. The doctor stated maybe the breech baby would eventually turn the right way, but if not, I would be ok. He expressed how close the babies were at each doctor's visit, indicating they would be extremely close twins and probably identical at birth.

CHAPTER 12:
SOON AFTER BIRTH

I gave birth to the boys on September 6, 1990. They were born 6 weeks early. They were in incubators at the hospital after birth for a week and after that, they were cleared to come home. They were healthy, alert, totally handsome and beautiful. I was so proud of them (happy that I had them). Having a child is one thing, but having twins was an amazement for me. They were mirror twins. One was left-handed, and the other one was right. One had a bow in his right leg and the other one had a bow in his left leg. One had a mole under the right titty on his chest and the other one to the left. They were identical twins, and they were inseparable.

Taking care of the boys didn't come hard, but certainly was not easy. My Madea helped me, but as the boys grew, they became a handful. When the boys were 5 months old, I moved out and got my first apartment. That didn't work so, I was back at my Madea's within a few months. By that time, the boys were receiving Supplemental Security Income (SSI) from their dad. One day he asked for a blood test and four months later, the boys were receiving a monthly check.

Soon after this, things went bad again.

CHAPTER 13:
STORE TRIP

By the time the boys were potty-trained and walking, I was using again. I remember it like it was yesterday.

My mom came over to Madea's house to get a beer and see the boys. Madea would always have beer as she drank it daily. When my mom sat down, Madea asked if she had a ride outside. Madea didn't have a car, so it was usual for her to send people to the store for beer and cigarettes. My mom said yes, and Madea gave her $20 and said, "Let Shon ride with you." The purpose of me riding was to make sure we came back. This was the very first time I left my boys for a week. We didn't come back, and I spent the entire SSI check on crack cocaine.

After this happened, I was leaving my boys with Madea regularly. One time I came back, and she had cut all their hair off and put it in a bag. I didn't have the courage to ask her why she did it. I just went along with it. I was coming in and out of Madea's house all different hours of the night and she would complain about it.

My mom and I often stayed there to rest after days of running the streets. We had a thing going, she would find the men and I would sleep with them. I was 18 years old selling my body for crack. I barely took care of myself. I caught a few STDs and was hospitalized for PID (pelvic inflammatory disease). The infection nearly killed me, and I was in the hospital for two weeks. The doctors stated they didn't understand how I was still functioning due to the severity of the infection.

CHAPTER 14:
CHANGE OF HEART

As I grew older in my addiction, I didn't want my mom finding men for me anymore. We would often argue over how much money they gave and how we were going to split the drugs. Something developed in my mind, *"Why was she getting anything, why was I splitting my drugs and money with her?"* Those days finally ended. I started running the streets without her.

One day she came up to me and said, "Shon, I got you somebody special, he got money, and he will give you everything you need." I said ok and allowed her to take me to him. Later he told me he had given her $50 to come get me. That was the most she ever got for pointing a guy in my direction. So, I was thinking, maybe he is the one. Maybe being with him would lessen all the activities I had going with these other men.

This guy was 42 years of age, married with 3 children from his wife and a child outside of his marriage. That didn't mean anything *at all* to me. My main concern was, *"Can he support my habit?"* He did a pretty good job of it. He also took care of my twins. He got me a place to stay and called me his main woman. So yes, there were other women, but he managed to make me feel special.

CHAPTER 15:
ADDICTION OVER FEAR

At the age of 20, I was arrested for the first time as an adult. I was charged with possession of cocaine and disturbing the peace. I had a big fight with the married guy in the parking lot of a motel. He found me there with another man and decided to slap me. We went a few rounds until the police showed up. When they got there, they found a crack pipe on me and took me to jail. My bond was set at $8000 but he bonded me out. When I went to court, I was sentenced to 2 years, but I only served 10 months and was free again.

After this incarceration, I signed up for low-income housing and got me an apartment. My guy friend was still helping me, coming over every night, and things were going smoothly. This was up until one day I decided to get high again. I was allowing people in and out of my apartment to smoke crack. I was also turning tricks (sleeping with men for money) in the daytime when my boys were asleep. Sometimes I would ask them to step outside and play.

This became a nightmare when I got pregnant again. I was not expecting that at all. This was not my intent. My addiction escalated at this time. I was using crack cocaine heavily during my pregnancy.

The fear of me having a baby addicted to cocaine with a handicap stayed on my mind, yet I could not control my usage. In fact, matters got worse. Before long, I was hospitalized. My lungs were full of fluid from smoking. I was hooked up to a machine, barely breathing, and they said I had asthma.

My body was going through a lot, and I didn't know if I would lose my baby or be able to ever breathe on my own again. Seven days later, I was well enough to be released. I went back to my apartment and the madness started all over again. This time I was pregnant and couldn't move around much, but I was still getting high.

CHAPTER 16:
SHOTS FIRED

In 1993, while I was pregnant with my daughter, the twins' father started visiting them every so often. He would come by the apartment, pick them up and take them for a ride in his convertible.

One day he pulled up in a different car and honked the horn for the boys to come out. As I got the boys ready, we heard gunshots fired. At the time, we didn't know what was going on. In our neighborhood we would hear the sound of gunfire often, but that didn't mean someone was injured. I told the boys to lock the front door. I was peeping out the window on one end and the twins on the other. It was a lot of commotion that day. People were running, crying and screaming. That alone scared us, as we wondered if anybody was hurt. We started to hear sirens and up the street came flashing lights. This is when we opened the door and eased down the stairs.

The car their father came in was parked across the street, but he was not in it. Someone ran up to us and called their dads name, indicating he had been shot. I looked across a field that was adjacent to my apartment. I saw an ambulance and, on the ground, laid his body. After the boys fully understood what happened, they cried in anger, and I could not contain them. They were kicking and screaming trying to run to the ambulance and calling their daddy's name.

At the age of 3, they lost their dad and by the time they were 6, I was full-blown in my addiction. In other words, both of us were absent in different ways. I went into labor on the day of the funeral, so I was unable to attend. I was told my younger son walked up to the casket and said, "Wake up Daddy." This was a sad occasion.

CHAPTER 17:
UNCHARTED TERRITORY

At the age of 21, I went to my first rehab. My daughter was 6 months old, and my boys were 3. So much had happened at this time, I just couldn't take anymore, so I decided to go into a 7-day detox program. After that, I admitted myself into a treatment facility. I was there for 30 days and left AMA (Against Medical Advice). I made one call, and that same married guy picked me up. Hours later, I was getting high. I just couldn't kick the habit. That vicious cycle started all over again.

Months later, I went to a halfway house. I didn't finish that program either. Time after time, I failed to stay sober. I knew something was wrong with me. I just couldn't figure it out. A few months after that, I reached out to a program for mothers and children. They provided health care and day care for single moms. They also rendered counseling for addiction disorders. Upon completing this program, they were offering low-income apartments in the projects. I successfully completed the program and got the apartment.

I was doing good, sending my kids to school, attending job education classes and looking for employment. The same married guy I was dating bought me a car. I was feeling independent at this time. I had not experienced responsibility on this level before, nor had I been sober this long. At this point, I had been with him 4 years, and honestly, I didn't know how to be with him without drugs. Our relationship was always based on that exchange, money or drugs for sex. Over time, I slipped back into my old behavior and started using again, but this time it was different. The conditions of keeping my apartment was based on my sobriety and compliance to the single moms' program.

CHAPTER 18:
THE BIG TAKE OVER

I was living in the projects for two years under a microscope and my reckless behavior finally came to an end. I was having regular visits from CPS and the school my kids were attending was calling at least once a week. I would miss their calls on purpose. One day the phone rang and woke me up out of my sleep. It was the school counselor telling me my daughter had walked to school with her brothers, but she was not enrolled. As I was sleeping, she decided to dress herself and walk to school with them without me knowing.

The only thing I could do was go get her and apologize. The faculty in the school office stared at me as I announced myself. Some of them smiled, but I could feel the awkwardness. I grabbed my daughter's hand and made my exit. I had so much going on. I was the talk of the projects. I sold my air conditioners out of the windows every other week. The guy I dated would bring another one to replace them. People were in and out of my apartment all day and night. Most times, I would leave my own apartment because I couldn't manage it. The project boys would gamble there and basically drive me out of my own place. I would owe four or five of them at a time in crack debt leaving them freedom to take over my apartment as they threatened me behind the money I owed. Things were out of control, but soon all of it would come to an end.

CHAPTER 19:
ON THE RUN

One morning at 2am, I left my kids at home alone and all hell broke loose. I said I was going to make a run and come right back. I was traveling across a bridge and when I got in the middle of it, my car ran out of gas. I put the car in *park*, sat there for a minute thinking, *what am I going to do?* There were no cars in sight. Minutes later, a van rear-ended me while I was in the car. He got out of the van and asked me why I didn't have my flashers on. Then he asked me if I was ok. The back of the car had a pretty good dent. We stood there as he called the police. In frustration, I left the car and the man there and started walking. A car picked me up maybe a mile into my walk. I never saw that car again.

As daylight came, I was thinking "I got to get home", but getting loaded was more important. I called that guy that I was dating and told him I was not home, the car was wrecked and for him to pick my kids up and take them to my Madea. He said ok. Between that phone call and later into the day, someone told me I was on the news. I asked them why and they replied, "Child abandonment." Apparently, my friend didn't pick the kids up. I called him and he said he thought I went home. He also said the police were looking for me to arrest me. I told him I was scared, and I knew, but I was going home. When I got there, the projects were surrounded with police, and I saw my children standing in protective custody with them and CPS. There were several news cameras. I couldn't face what was happening. I didn't get out of the car. I told the driver to keep going.

CHAPTER 20:
A MAD WORLD

In 1996, at the age of 24, I had my first nervous breakdown. I was battling multiple personalities, bipolar disorder, manic depression and substance abuse disorder. The thought of leaving my kids and losing them tore me completely apart. I beat myself down for that. Not to mention, I was not quite over the trauma of my childhood and past experiences. Covered in pain, guilt and regret, I found ways to medicate myself, digging a deeper hole of shame. I was drowned in sorrow and couldn't see my way out. I was mad at the world and blamed everybody for my problems. A day didn't go by where either I wished I was dead or that everybody would just die around me.

I was going back and forth to court on child desertion charges. They were allowing me to see my kids through CPS. Each time I would leave them, they would yell and cry for me. I would be crying, and this would intensify my sadness, leaving me feeling worse. I would think to myself, *"Did my babies feel as bad as I did?"* I couldn't wrap my mind around how I would rise above all that happened and get sober long enough to get them back. I didn't know how to fight, nor did I know how to stay sober.

CPS assigned me a caseworker, who would walk me through the steps of getting my kids back. She was there to assist me and guide me through this process. The first step was getting me clean. I got into a 90-day program and successfully completed it. After that, I got back into school and got my GED. That same married guy I was dating got me a house and a car, and I started working.

CHAPTER 21:
LET'S TAKE A DRINK

I hadn't felt this good in a long time. I was employed at the casino working for a nice restaurant as a Salad Prep. This establishment sold steak, expensive wine and other foods. The atmosphere was good, and the employees were great. They often invited me to their homes or engagements for gatherings. I went once or twice but kept my distance knowing I couldn't party as they did because I was an addict. I was also fighting a case to get my kids back, but they didn't know this. They didn't know I was an addict either. They would offer me drinks, but I would always decline.

I was on a 90-day probation period with my new job, going to meetings and taking random UAs with my case manager. Everything seemed to be going fine. I was talking to my kids throughout the week as we all anticipated weekend visits once I got the approval through CPS. My kids were with a family in Cotton Valley. I lived in Shreveport, so we were one hour and a half away from each other.

After 63 days on my job, I was approved for the weekend visits. My kids were coming home two weekends out of the month. That same married guy I was dating, and I would go pick them up on Fridays when I got off work. This was a happy time for us all, yet a sensitive moment. I didn't fully understand what was going on in their minds as children, but I had a lot of fears going on in mine. My deepest fear was whether could I be a mother. I didn't have that confidence. Moreover, this man that was in my life who was said to be the father of my daughter was helping me, but on a part-time basis, because "he" had a family.

I am not sure what my family was thinking. None of us had ever been involved with CPS, nor had we encountered this type of experience. It was odd and to be honest, I didn't feel getting my kids back would be a success. I was contemplating defeat before I acquired victory. I remember on our second visit, one of my sons had an episode. He fought his brother over a game and went into a rage all over the house. I grabbed him, held him down and yelled these words, "I am going to send you back to those people if you keep this up." He cried so much after I said that till it opened something in me, and I begin to cry. I realized I had said something that ripped my son's heart out and the sound of it was disturbing and affected us all.

When we packed that Sunday to go back, my other son asked, "Mom, are you going to let us come back?" That hurt me even more. I said, "Sure son" and apologized again. All of us were saddened by the statement I made. Little did I know, they were in a battle too. We took them home that Sunday, and the entire car was filled with silence. I went on a guilt trip after that and slowly fell apart from all the progress that was made.

I went to work later that day. During work, a female co-worker asked me if I was ok. I didn't go into detail, but I told her I was not. She said, "Girl, you probably need a drink." They all drank sociably, even while working. At the time when she said it, I knew one drink would send me further than I wanted to go, but the possibility that 'one drink wouldn't hurt' stuck in my mind. I deviated from my path of recovery which was total abstinence and considered having one drink after work. Even while working, the anticipation grew and I began to feel better in my emotions from the incident with my son.

"One drink won't hurt" was the biggest lie I told myself. After work, I agreed to go have drinks. In my mind, I would have one drink and ease on to the house and experience this relapse alone instead of getting drunk with my coworkers. After all, I was a smoker. One drink would only lead me to getting high.

This particular night, I went home and went to work the next day. It felt like I had escaped having a full-blown episode, which was going out and finding the dope man after drinking. I was proud of myself and justified that one drink didn't hurt me after all.

CHAPTER 22:
FALSE COURAGE

My kids were coming home on the first and third weekends. As we approached the second weekend visit, which was our second time visiting, I got high again. I didn't come home after work. I took a drink after work and ended up hanging out all night getting high from crack cocaine, knowing my kids were home for the weekend and they were waiting for me.

I finally mustered up the courage to go home. I walked in the door with a 40-ounce beer in my hand and sat down. My younger son, Trenton, walked into the living room and touched me on my shoulder and asked me if I was ok. I began to cry and so did he. The next day we packed up and took the kids back.

I didn't get much rest the night before and everybody involved knew I had relapsed except CPS. We all agreed not to tell them. We called it a slip, but in my heart, I knew I would do it again. I didn't feel like stopping. I really felt like giving up. So, the next day I went to work knowing I wouldn't have my job long. I was two weeks away from my 90-day probation period and by that time, my kids would be back home for another weekend.

I attended a few AA meetings during this time after work hours and gleamed a little hope. As the weekend approached to get my kids, I began to feel anxious, contemplating our visit and how it would be. I was just going through the motions. In my mind I had chosen getting high over being with my children. In that moment, it felt like the easiest thing to do. That Friday, I stayed with them. Saturday night after they went to bed, I left. I returned early Sunday morning with a beer in my hand, too high and embarrassed to take them back. My boyfriend took them back by himself and told CPS I had relapsed and that was the reason why I was not present on the return.

The judge ended my visits until further notice and ordered me to go to weekly meetings. I took the liberty to go back to school to get my GED and attend weekly meetings. In my mind, I would go above and beyond and get it over with. Maybe they would leave us alone. I was reporting to CPS regularly preparing to see the judge. The day of court, my case manager reported to the judge that I had gotten my GED and attended AA meetings, but he stated I needed more time sober before they resume the weekend visits. I walked away from court feeling empty and defeated. Another slap in the face; and as you are guessing, I went and got high.

I missed court twice after this and when I finally showed up, the judge terminated my parental rights. This was another major breaking point. I didn't expect this, nor was I ever told terminating my parental rights was an option. So, this decision took me by surprise. I didn't see it coming. They also terminated the rights of my daughter's father, stating he had her out of wedlock. He didn't see it coming, as he painted himself as the good parent and me as the bad one.

I couldn't believe my ears, nor could I wrap my mind around what had happened. I had no legal rights to my children; our relationship would no longer exist and usually the parents had no right to visit or talk with the children. My name would be removed from their birth certificates, and they could be adopted without my consent. I found this process out years later, but that day when I walked away from that court room, I didn't know what terminating my parental rights truly meant in its totality and honestly, I wasn't trying to find out.

I had gotten what I deserved, and my children would be better off without me. This is what I told myself to avoid responsibility as a mother and excuse all the ways I had failed at being a good parent. I walked away with no hope, full of regrets. I knew I had lost the battle I was fighting to get my children back, but I was at war with finding myself, getting me back.

Losing them was one thing, but I had lost me. Imagine being in a fight or battle without knowing who you are. The only thing I knew and the only comfort I could find was in getting high. Self-medicating was the only answer I had.

CHAPTER 23:
BROKEN CHAINS

A couple of months later, I lost the house I was living in and sold everything in it. My life was reduced to living on the streets or in motels. I never returned to the job I had. I was back to walking the streets, car hopping, spending days in dope houses and hustling crack. This lifestyle became a norm for me and a way for me to cope. Between the ages of 25 and 37, I was lost. I wandered the streets living anywhere I could. I would stay in hotels and journey to different parts of the city because I was in so much mischief. Bouncing from one neighborhood to the other because I would be burned out, hiding from people for one reason or the other.

I caught two possession charges and was locked up a couple of times, but managed to get out. I served 10 months on two-year sentences twice for possession of cocaine. During these years, I was also hospitalized on several occasions and placed on the psych ward due to nervous breakdowns. During one of those trips, I became a ward of the state. They held me there against my will due to mental illness. One morning, I woke up chained to the bed and later put in a straitjacket to protect others from me and me from myself. Can you imagine the humiliation and pain that I felt? The pretty girl I once knew who was smart in school, known for cheerleading was strapped to a bed in a psych ward. I would battle with the thoughts of losing myself and my children. How could I bounce back from all this? Would I die in this state of mind? Would my life end this way, or could God save "me"?!!

While lying there in that hospital bed heavily medicated, I would hum hymns that I remembered as a child. My mom would sing them in my hearing at church. The medication would calm me one way, but those hymns would bring me a peace of mind that I couldn't fully explain at the time. I remember one nurse telling another nurse that I could sing. One afternoon, I was awake when they came into my room. They asked me to sing, and I did. They began to cry. And of course, I cried too. The doctor walked in and saw all of us crying and he walked out. After the song, one of them grabbed my hand and told me to pray, and the other one confirmed it with a nod of her head. They gathered themselves and left me in the room alone. This experience eased my mind and gave me hope.

Upon my release from the hospital, a case manager came into my room as part of my discharge assessment. I learned the hospital had filed for my SSI and my next step would be making the appointment so I could receive benefits. In all honesty, I was triggered by this information and the first thing that came to my mind was I had a 'for sure way' to get high. I was anxious to leave the hospital, make the appointment and follow up. In less than 90 days, I was getting SSI benefits.

CHAPTER 24:
SICK AND TIRED

At the age of 37, I was declared mentally ill and was to spend the rest of my life as a ward of the state. I felt like my role as a mother, daughter, family member or even a person had ended. I think this had a lot to do with my battle, the roller coaster of pain and my final decision to give up. I wasn't dead, but I felt like it. I never thought I would be so crazed out of my mind. I walked around and lived my life as a bum getting a check on the 1st of the month, spending it all on crack cocaine before the next day. I didn't know these were my final days of getting high, but I knew I was tired. Not just tired of getting high, but tired of living an inhumane and dreadful life.

CHAPTER 25:
NOT MY WAY

On May 11, 2011, at the age of 38, I was arrested. I was sitting on a milk cart in front of an abandoned house talking to a few other drifters, drinking on a hot beer. Two guys pulled up in a white Crown Vic got out of the car and walked over to us. They asked if anybody had any weed. We all said "No." One of them looked at me and asked if I knew anybody and I said yes. I got up and left with them. When we got into the car, we gained an understanding that I would get them weed if they gave me money for crack. They agreed and gave me $20 dollars.

I proceeded to take them to the house where we would score. When we got there, I went inside and made my way out in 3 minutes. By that time, cops were everywhere. I was arrested for Distribution and taken to jail. Neither the drugs nor the money was mine, but I was detained. No one ever heard my side of the story. During my day in court, I was unable to speak. A state-appointed attorney spoke for me. It all happened so fast. The judge gave me two choices, either take 15 years or be multi-billed and take 20 years to life. The fact that I was declared mentally ill never came up in court. I believe justice was not served. The reality for me until this day, is that God used this incident to save my life. I took the 15 years and walked away feeling different and lighter. I wasn't worried. It was my "day of reckoning." The entire process felt like I had been rescued. Oddly, yet strange, I felt like I had a chance at life.

CHAPTER 26:
WELCOME TO LIFE

Two weeks later, I was sentenced to serve my time at LCIW (Louisiana Correctional Institute for Women), one of the largest prisons In Louisiana. A week after that, I was transferred to a satellite camp in Tallulah, L.A., where I would be housed until LCIW was ready to accept more people. There were fifteen other women on that bus with me. We were instructed not to talk during transport. The ride was filled with silence. No one said a mumbling word. We were chained in couples, as this was protocol for transporting convicts. It is common for satellite prisons to house inmates until openings were available at the main prison.

I was on a four-hour ride thinking about the road behind me and the journey ahead. I had lost everything and everybody. My great-grandmother, grandmother and my mom were deceased. My children had been taken away. The guy that I dated for 19 years, who was a constant in my life had died. I had nothing but the state-issued clothes on my back and a pair of run-over shoes on my feet. The most important person I lost was me.

We arrived at LTCW, (Louisiana Transitional Center for Women) around noon. The prison guards unloaded us off the bus and walked us through the gates. We went into a large area that was called the "visitation room." They gave us brown bags with a sandwich and chips and soon after that, they started separating us and putting us into dorms where we would be housed during the duration of our stay, or until we transferred to LCIW.

I wasn't excited to be there, but I didn't feel like I was in a bad environment. The inmates were working, getting us settled in, as the guards gave them orders. Before long, we were in our dorms. I didn't know how I was going to make it through this. Looking forward or behind, I did not have the family, resources or support to live within these walls comfortably. I did know there were rules I had to follow as an inmate, and there would be consequences if I decided not to. I immediately found out what I needed to get a job, and 90 days after that, I was working. I didn't get paid to work, but it kept me busy and showed me I had skills. Eventually, I was working three jobs to make sure I had something to do seven days a week. I soon learned I enjoyed working and this is how I served my sentence.

CHAPTER 27:
ANOTHER CHANCE

Three and a half years passed, and I had not been transferred to the main prison (LCIW). In fact, my earned credits had put me on the waiting list to be accepted for Work Release. I was screened July 7, 2014, and transported the following month to Lake Charles Work Release Facility.

This was my first experience back into society. I had fears, but I was not afraid. My anxiety level was not as high as I once knew it to be. I was confident that I would not fail, yet uncertain of how I would adapt to being in a less secure environment. Honestly, I was looking for triggers, in the event my body didn't respond well. I was still incarcerated, but this was a new level of freedom. I was being very cautious, as it was in my best interest to keep my sanity and protect my recovery.

Work Release offered transportation, jobs and classes. They also had a kitchen which served breakfast, lunch and dinner. It was a healthy and safe environment. I had no complaints about it. Their rules were easy to follow, and I saw myself being there until my release date. My plans were to work, save money and move to Lake Charles when all of this was over. I never wanted to go back to my hometown, and this was my chance to relocate.

I didn't start working immediately after getting there. Several women were shipped to the facility and jobs were not available before screening. We soon learned there were more women than jobs. We were given permission to contact employers within a certain mile radius to assist them in finding us employment. They had contracts with a few establishments that paid well.

These companies were of high preference because of the pay rate, but the facility was careful in who they chose to go on certain sites due to flight risk or lack of job training. I was there six weeks before I started working. In the meantime, I focused on a daily schedule of learning the staff and facility, doing assigned chores and participating in group activities. One day as I was stirring around, there was a lot of commotion at the tech station. A new list had come out with 12 names on it to work for one of the biggest companies they were in contract with. The tech was calling out the names and I was one of them.

This was a nine-month contract. I worked 10-hour shifts, 6 days a week and sometimes we were on 7 days. After the facility took out room and board, I came out pretty good. I kept a personal ledger and balanced my earnings each week. They kept a record as well and would pass them out to us weekly.

One day I noticed our numbers were not the same. Over one thousand dollars was missing from my account. I requested a meeting with the program director. He was very polite until he found out why I was in his office. His tone changed, but he corrected the issue.

I walked away feeling uneasy. I monitored my finances even more and discovered another mishap one month later. I was back in his office again pointing out the same error and he corrected it again. The energy between us was not good. In my opinion, he talked to me as if I was a smarty pants, but in all honesty, I was uncomfortable presenting the problem to him. In my mind, if this was an error, let's fix it and move forward. This was my second encounter with him. I did not know it would be the third one that sent me back to prison.

CHAPTER 28:
CAN'T GIVE UP NOW

A year was approaching, and the contract with my job was ending. It was time to find another job. It didn't happen suddenly. The employer informed us 30 days ahead. That would give us time to find more work, as they knew we were in work release. I started looking for employment before the contract ended and the facility was looking too. They found me a placement at a hotel. Three months into working for the hotel, I inquired about a second job to supplement for the earnings I was not making after losing my first one. They agreed, as it was customary to work two jobs after being in the program for six months.

One day as we were headed back to the facility, we stopped at a restaurant to pick up a few ladies. One of them had told me this workplace was hiring, and I should inquire with the supervisor, and she would give her my name. I was so excited. I asked the driver if I could exit the van to check on a job. She said, "Make it quick". I spoke to the supervisor, she took my name and said she would give the facility a call to hire me.

Two weeks later while I was at work at the hotel, upper management called me downstairs and said the van was there to pick me up. Instantly I thought something was wrong. When I got back to the property, the program director and employment facilitator had a meeting set up for me. They charged me with "simple escape" for getting off the van to inquire about a job and made arrangements to send me back to prison. I didn't have the words to ask for a second chance, although they made it clear the decision was already made.

As they walked me out in chains, I didn't drop my countenance. I held my head high and walked out with dignity. Although I was filled with embarrassment, I smiled and said my goodbyes to the ladies I was leaving behind.

They didn't ship me to the satellite camp where I came from. I was transported to LCIW (Louisiana Corrections Institute for Women) where I would serve and complete the remainder of my sentence. That was the last time I was handcuffed to this very day.

CHAPTER 29:
GET A GRIP

Here I was, back in prison. Most would call this a mistake, a fall, a disappointment or moving backwards. I called it an opportunity to grow, expand and reach my full potential. I was yet hopeful and saw myself as making progress. I said to myself, *"Well Lord, I won't be living in Lake Charles"*, cause if you remember, I was thinking after work release, I would move there. Anyway, I never went to lock down for the "simple escape" charge. It was reviewed and immediately thrown out due to lack of evidence. I was informed I could appeal the write-up, but I was not interested. I had 16 months before my release and knew the process would take longer than I had left. By the time I won the appeal, my sentence would be nearly over.

This is where I say "God's divine timing and our timing are not the same. No matter how hard we try, things may not go the way we planned, but in the end because we put forth an effort, we are acknowledged as a person who thrived and not a person who gave up. Everything happens for a reason, in which at the time we don't understand. We may say "Why is this happening to me?", but ultimately the answers are revealed later. In these moments, we must trust a being higher than ourselves and know our purpose in life is bigger than any mishap or mistake we've made. In saying this, we must learn to move forward, stay the course and run the race that has been set before us.

With 16 months left, I knew I had to do three things; pray, work and keep going. I put in for one of the most prominent jobs on the compound, which was the garment factory. Of course, there was picking grass, doing laundry, wiping the walls down and a few others, but I thought this job would better suit me. I was hired in the packaging division. My duties were shipping and handling. I reported to work at 4am, so this means I was up praying at 3. I was still intimate with God as I knew and felt in my heart that He was my only Comforter, Helper and Friend. In spite of those times when I let myself down and made bad decisions, He was there to get me through. And right now, I want to say, "Thank you Lord for Your All-Sufficient Grace!"

CHAPTER 30:
THE FLOOD

Ten months later, on August 30, 2016, the prison flooded. We heard the commotion that the water was covering the grounds. The prison guards were ordering all inmates to report to their living quarters and remain stationed. At first, no one knew where the water was coming from. We later learned the levee broke. The water was steady rising. They ordered all inmates to pack two small bags, and if we had boots, we should put them on. We all were running wild complaining about our belongings. Many of us had acquired quite a bit over the years; and for some, the prison was considered home. So, we were leaving a lot behind. Everybody was asking where they were going and how they would get the things they were leaving. The staff didn't have answers because this had never happened before. They gathered us all in a common area as they sorted through our names to send us to different facilities. At some point, they ran out of chains to join us together and just started sending us to the buses to get us out of there. Imagine over 1000 women being shipped at one time to different locations. I was transported back to the satellite camp where my sentence first started. Surprisingly, when they saw me, everyone was curious to know why I was discharged from work release. Partially embarrassed, I explained. A couple of days later, I asked if they would consider giving me one of my old jobs back to keep me busy. A week later, I was working with only 6 months left in my sentence.

CHAPTER 31:
A PATH FOR ME

The month of January in 2017, I began to consecrate myself. I was seeking God for guidance about my release. I never wanted to go to jail or prison. I always had this fear of going. However, the experience of being there gave me security. I felt safe. Being inside those walls gave me a sense of protection. Truthfully, I did not know how I would function in society. I wasn't even sure if I could make it in the free world.

More days into my consecration, my fears lessened, and God gave me direction. By the 15th day of my consecration, He brought into my remembrance the story of Abraham. He is the father of many nations. He was summoned by God to leave his country and his people.

(Genesis 12:1-3 Now the Lord said unto Abram, "Go out from your country, your relatives, and your father's household to a land I will show you. Then I will make you a great nation, and I will bless you, and I will make your name great, so that you will exemplify divine blessing. I will bless those who bless you, but the ones who treats you lightly I must curse, so that all the families of the earth may receive blessings through you.)

Above all this, Abraham believed God. So, there were two things I had to do after my release; the first thing was to believe God, and the second thing was to leave my relatives and hometown to dwell amongst strangers.

Time was winding down rather quickly. I was 90 days short from being released. I knew what I had to do concerning my journey to another state, but at the time I didn't know where I would be going. It settled in my heart to take one step at a time. The first step was, where would I go upon my release?

I had not talked to my intermediate family in years. My only point of contact back home was the stepdad who molested me. Early on during my incarceration, he apologized for his actions, and over time, the support he showed, compared to "none at all", was appreciated.

Two weeks before my release I mustered up the courage to ask him if I could stay with him until my Interstate Compact was approved. He said yes. At this time, I still didn't know what state I was transferring my parole to, but I knew I was leaving, and things would pan out.

April 17, 2017, I was released from prison. This day was the end of my incarceration, but the beginning of me breaking the chains of imprisonment. In other words, I had to relearn how to be free. They escorted me in a van to the bus station. I purchased a ticket to get home and was given a card with my remaining balance from inmate banking.

CHAPTER 32:
THE LAST STRAW

We arrived at his house. I had one bag to carry. I packed light, as I gave most of my things to the ladies I left behind. He showed me my room and spoke with welcoming words. I was hesitant, but his words did not match his energy. Another reason for me to seek God for direction, as I knew in that moment I wouldn't be there long. I recognized his intentions right away. His spirit did not sit well with me. Instead of entertaining his thoughts, I isolated myself in prayer. It settled in my heart to set boundaries and keep a distance from him. I would speak to him out of respect, but I never engaged in long conversations. Around the fifth day he stated, "What did they do to you, you've changed, and you don't talk much?" I replied, "I must keep quiet so I can hear from God." He took that one statement to challenge me on how much I knew about God and said to me he didn't believe I could hear from God. That day, I knew my time was running out to be there. The following day he came into my room and stated I needed to "keep the door open at all times". That disturbed my peace completely. I instantly felt violated and knew I had to leave.

He had given me a phone and told me I could use it long as I was there. I called my Auntie and within 5 minutes she was outside honking her horn repetitively. I grabbed that one bag, gave him his phone, and preceded to walk out the front door. His last words to me were, "You're not going to make it." I shook my head and said with a smile, "Thanks for everything."

As we drove away, she had a few choice words for him, and I quickly changed the subject with telling her how glad I was to see her. She agreed and we started conversations.

I went to my aunt's house for a few days and a week later I was staying with my cousin. I had been gone a long time and when I left, she was only 23 years old with an apartment, but now she owned her own home, and she invited me to stay. It warmed my heart the way she asked. Her invite was pure with no ill will or intent. She gave me a room and stated it was mine long as I needed it to be. The atmosphere was safe. The energy in the home was positive. I was able to pray and meditate unbothered. She had three children, which she managed well. They were very respectful. The younger one is a girl, who tended to come into my room and check on me. She had to be 2 or 3 years old. One specific time, she came into my room and caught me crying and cried with me. She gave me a few soft pats on my back, which felt like a touch of encouragement.

CHAPTER 33:
ALL IN A DREAM

Two weeks was approaching, and I was seeking an answer. I needed to know what state I was transferring to, so I could tell my parole officer. I was meeting him or her for the first time. I reported 72 hours after my release, but they told me to come back in two weeks. I was told that rarely happens. I walked away thinking, *I will have an answer on which state when I get back.*

After a week or so, I had a dream about a time when we did a family trip to Houston, TX. We would go there often before I became a teenager. When I woke up, I was thinking about my relatives there. I looked up one of them on Facebook, we exchanged numbers and I gave her a call. We talked for hours and shared childhood memories. I spoke to her about my quest to leave Louisiana and she gave me the phone number of another family member who worked at a homeless shelter for women and children. She explained that the cousin who worked at this place could help me get an apartment. I gave her a call and learned I would have to live in the shelter to receive housing. I knew this would be a journey and I was ready for it. In my mind, I had been to hospitals, mental institutions, jails and prisons.

How bad could living in a homeless shelter be? They were people just like me. What could go wrong?

Before I went to prison, I was receiving Social Security Disability. I applied after my release to ensure I would have some type of income to support my mission. I was aware I wouldn't have it long, as I knew I would gain employment sooner than later. Over the years, I had grown accustomed to working.

Two weeks later, I was at the parole office prepared to pay my Interstate Compact fees. Meeting my parole officer for the first time and soon to be the last. I had seen her one more time after my paperwork was finalized. It took one month to complete the process.

CHAPTER 34:
WHERE IS YOUR MIRACLE?

June 29, 2017, I was headed to Houston on a Greyhound Bus. A one-way ticket with no reservations of looking back or going back. It was set in my heart that a new life was waiting for me. I was sure everything and anything I needed or wanted was ahead of me. Leaving was a bittersweet moment, but I had to go.

When I arrived at the bus station in Houston, my aunt and cousin were there to pick me up. My plan was to stay with relatives until a bed was available at the shelter, and that's what I did. I made the necessary calls and kept updates on bed openings. A week later, July 5, 2017, I was admitted into the shelter. My relatives invited me to their homes, but this was the route I chose to take. God told me to go to a land I did not know and dwell amongst strangers. I needed to be around people I didn't know. I understood familiarity would give me a level of comfort that would hinder my progress and deactivate my faith. Besides, my obedience would determine my destiny.

The shelter provided housing, drug treatment, case management, bus passes, food, clothing and a host of support groups for stabilization. I was careful in choosing from what they had to offer and the programs I would participate in. I narrowed my choices down to church, housing, bus passes and job search. Seven days a week, I distributed my time to one or the other. I'd wake up early in the morning and get my day started. I rode city buses or the metro-rail all over Houston, and most days, especially in the beginning, I would get lost.

In less than 30 days, I was working at McDonalds. A week later, I got a second job at Griff's Burgers. Working two jobs was easy. The bus lines were the same, and my schedules were compatible. I would leave one job and go to the next. By 9pm, I would be finished.

Meanwhile as I worked, I applied for a housing voucher, enrolled in college and started my search for transportation. Having a car would make life much easier. Houston was big. The bus commute took up a lot of time, and I knew school would be starting soon. I trained myself to prepare while I wait.

November 3, 2017, I purchased a car from Dallas, TX. It was delivered to me November 11, ten days before my birthday. The following week my voucher was approved for housing. I had found an apartment prior to all this happening and spoke to the apartment manager. She was waiting, and so was I for the certification to come through. Here I was, moving into an apartment with two jobs and a car, days after my birth date.

CHAPTER 35:
LOOKING FOR LOVE

January 13, 2018, was the first day of school. My schedule was full. I decided to let my part-time job go, so I could find balance. McDonalds was all for education and allowed me to have a flexible schedule. I would work overnight two days out the week, one evening shift, and two mornings. I did this my first year of school and made changes along the way, but never skipped a beat. Some asked how I did it, and others were doing the same exact thing. So, I surrounded myself with those who did. Generally, it was my classmates. We all worked and went to school.

During my first full year in Houston, I accomplished much, but I was eager to build a relationship with my children. I wasn't sure how to, but I tried in the ways I could. Mainly, this was reaching out by calls or text. I would also get travel passes from my parole officer to go see them back home. Secondly, I wanted to get to know my grandchildren and their parents. Not only that, but I also desired for all of them to learn me too. All of this was difficult in the beginning, but as time grew, the communication lines were easier. We were developing a connection and growing. I was still experiencing rebellion from my daughter, but I figured she needed more time, and I was understanding of that. I learned a valuable lesson during these times, that money and materialistic things may help, but they do not fix relationships or families. I discovered how broken we were as a family unit, and how great the dysfunction was.

After being absent for so long, where would I start? I didn't know any of them. As for my children, all they knew of me is that I was the crackhead mom who left them. To them, whatever they experienced apart from me was my fault. How they responded to me was a strong indication of this. I was treated as if I owed them something or as if I was in debt to them. It was always about what I could do for them and what I had to offer. Our conversations were always surrounded by what they needed. What happened to the calls or texts for them to check on me? With my grandchildren, it was different. They were not adults charging me for lost times. They were young babes, who enjoyed being in my presence. We had fun. Their energy towards me was lighthearted, sincere and unapologetic. Their love was unconditional. My time spent with them kept me steady, brought balance to my disappointment and healing to my broken heart.

Over a course of time, I learned my children didn't get along. I notice how they spoke ill of one another in a harsh way. My daughter didn't have anything good to say about her brothers and the twins were a touch worse, constantly battling, at odds with one another, having nothing good to say about each other. It wasn't the norm. I've seen siblings go at it, but this was different. In my opinion, they didn't like each other. I thought in my mind, *how did it get this way*? I began to question them on how they were brought up in my absence, seeking out answers to how they evolved into this hate relationship. Where did it stem from?

I thought about a few things as I sought out answers. *I deserted them. Did they take out their abandonment issues on one another?* I never taught them how to love. Was that the issue? We were separated while they were young. Could this be a factor? I did not know what to think. They all stated on several occasions that their adopted parents treated them differently than they did their birth son. Could this be it? Or was it just several things compiled together to produce this hostility.

CHAPTER 36:
I NEEDED ME

April 17, 2018, made a full year of me being home. I had accomplished much but had two years left to complete school with my associate degree and obtain my license. I would look back over my progress and this encouraged me to keep going. I was close to finishing my first semester in school and was very proud. There were a few things I had to do for myself to assure me I could make it. I had goals and aspirations, but my main objective was to fully equip myself for the journey ahead. I knew God saved my life for a reason, but I had to find out what it was. My development was important, and I had to make sure my mind was focused. I faced the reality that before I went to prison, my life was upside-down, filled with chaos and trauma. I didn't know how to live back then, and I didn't take it for granted that being in prison over six years taught me how. I didn't assume I would be alright. I had to work toward it. My perspective was set in stone. I needed to build and reevaluate my entire way of thinking. I took my time, asked for help and remained humble. I was mindful how I received provision and careful in where my guidance came from.

As a mother, it was natural for me to be concerned about my children. The heaviness of how and why I deserted them never left me. At the moment, of losing them, I was grieved. Even in my addiction, the thoughts would occur and torment me. Losing them was one thing, but how it would be if I got them back stayed on my mind. Even when my parental rights were terminated, this conception never left me. As I got sober, the desire was there, but my perspective changed. I no longer wanted to get clean for them, but for myself. I accepted the fact that they were adults with children of their own. I couldn't go back in time and change things, and neither could I change them.

CHAPTER 37:
NO MORE LOSSES

The year of 2018, I made arrangements with my parole officer to travel back home every 90 days to visit my family. They explained they never do this in such a short time frame, but made an exception for me. I proved myself to be trustworthy and followed their rules with diligence. I paid my parole fees up for a year and made it to my appointments on time.

My main objective was to reunite with my children and grandchildren. I didn't expect it to happen overnight, nevertheless I had expectations that we would gradually come together. The more I went, the more I was able to understand how everyone communicated, which was little or "none at all". I saw my sons together on one occasion, and my daughter once at a store she worked at. I have eight grandchildren, but at the time, I could only see six. I was seeing everyone separately, but never together. Occasionally, I would suggest we all should get together, but it never happened. My sons were generally beefed out and my daughter kept her distance.

It was one thing to lose my children while they were young, but to lose them while they were adults was not the same encounter. For many years I thought, *"if only I could get better"* we would be ok. It never occurred to me that if I got sober, it wouldn't heal them nor would it help them get through the trauma they had experienced. We all went through things alone and other things together. My recovery was an indication that I had been treated, not them. In my opinion, they were still affected by our separation emotionally and mentally. Did they have any opportunities to recover or be healed? I don't know. Was the pain so deep that they couldn't or didn't know how to get past it? I can't deliberate. Because of these things, did they respond to life through the eyes of shame, embarrassment, fear, anger, guilt and defeat? These are speculations and questions that are yet to be answered; and to be honest, I still don't have a full understanding, but I will continue to trust the process.

As painful as it was, I had to accept my children had created a life in my absence that did not include me. I grew tired of the rejection and embraced the fact that they didn't have the same idea in mind that I did to reunite. I moved passed the thought and decided to let things be. In doing this, I practiced the rule of thumb, "Let go and let God." I had done my part, now it was time for me to let Him do His. Nevertheless, I had to let them be who they were. They weren't kids anymore; they were adults with lives of their own.

What happens when you don't get what you prayed for? How does it look, or how does it feel when matters get worse instead of getting better? The last quarter of 2018, nothing was going according to plan, yet I stayed hopeful and remained in prayer. I was in school, continued to study and kept working. My twin sons were at war, and it was reported to me that the "both of them" were on a powerful street drug called meth. I was surprised by this, because to my understanding my younger twin was working as a store manager and had gotten married. On the other hand, the older twin was a street hustler, but I never knew him to succumb to an influential drug such as this. At the same time, both were fighters and had the potential to take a life. They often displayed anger and took matters into their own hands.

One late evening after work, I received a call from jail. It was my youngest twin. He had been arrested for robbery at his place of employment. He never admitted to me that he did it, but the police believed it was him and his twin brother. He was released a couple of months later, and somehow this ignited the confusion between the brothers, because his twin believed he gave his name up to be released from jail. I did not know if this was true or not until the very day. This started mass confusion between the two.

CHAPTER 38:
NOT READY YET

Approaching my second year of school, January 2019, things got hectic. I was getting calls left and right concerning my twins. I was told the confusion between them had gotten worse. I had reason to believe that a few people were trying to get one brother to get rid of the other. I won't get into the different stories that were told, but I do know the younger twin was being blamed for a few things he denied. I planned for the younger twin to visit me in Houston. He was on parole, so he could only stay a week. I planned for him to come back periodically during these trying times, but he failed the first drug screen when he returned and was unable to come back until he was clean.

In our time alone, he stated that his twin brother and adopted family were plotting to kill him. He also conveyed they were planning to split his life insurance. I was in disbelief and questioned him for hours trying to figure out if this was true. The information shared put me in an awkward position. How could I stop them if it were true? What was the next best thing to do? If I told the police, I had no proof. The only other thing I could think of was to call them separately to confirm or deny the accusations. They all stated his allegations were far from the truth.

It was later told to me by the older twin that the younger twin was a drug informant, and because of that, the younger twin was in fear of his life. I asked my younger twin if this was true. He said yes and would rather move to Texas, because the people in which he worked for were not protecting him as they promised.

So much was being said at the time, I didn't know who or what to believe. It was a progression of confusion filled with multiple events leading up to a tragic end.

I made provisions to take a trip back home the first weekend of March 2019. My intention was to get the twins together, so we could straighten things out. They would talk to me individually but would not agree to come together. In my conversation with them, I learned a few things. Both had a posture of regret, as if life had failed them. They were commenting on failures and how they didn't get things right. Both were hurting, I could see it in their eyes. To my understanding, they were disappointed in each other, but they still loved one another deeply. In my mind, things would work themselves out and this would blow over.

As I got packed, ready to head back to Houston, I received a phone call from my younger son. He asked me to pick him up from his wife's house. When I got there, he was in a rage. He stated that they argued, and she had put him out. I stood there and watched him pack his things in a trash bag as I began to cry. My question was, "Son where are you going?" He answered and said, "I don't know." This was "definitely" a dilemma. I was on parole. He was on parole. If I had taken him home with me, we both would have gotten new charges, as we lived in different states.

I offered him a motel room, but he didn't want to go. He asked me to take him to the house. This didn't sit well with me because the house in the country belonged to the adopted family. He made a call and spoke to the adopted brother, and he agreed that he could come. When we arrived, I blew the horn, and he came out to greet us. He spoke to me and said to my son, "You good bro." My son stepped out of the car, gave me a hug, and saw me on my way.

I drove away thinking why would he go around the same people he said was against him. Then I thought about myself and all the bad decisions I made when my choices were slim to none. I didn't feel good about leaving him there and certainly didn't know that was the last time I would see him alive.

CHAPTER 39:
APRIL SHOWERS

When I returned home, I felt myself drifting into powerlessness. I was empty. As I unpacked my luggage, I thought to myself, *"I have never seen anything like this before."* Frankly, I had done all I know to do. I repeated to myself "God's Grace is sufficient." I ran out of ways to fight. I was burnt out from listening to so much chaos sending me in circles with no reprieve.

In the month of April 2019, I was getting more calls than usual. It was either the mom or son of the adopted family, the twins, or the people they knew. I took heed of the calls and listened, but I didn't have much to say anymore. Each time the phone rang, I thought it would be bad news.

On one occasion my younger son called and said he was having a baby. I hadn't heard his voice that cheerful in a long time. It made me happy because he was happy. Otherwise, the calls were usually aired in confusion.

April 29, 2019, while working the mid-shift at McDonald's, I received a text from the adopted mom requesting me to call her. She said it was urgent. I was taking orders at the back window. I hurriedly stepped away for a moment to make the call. She stated calmly that Trevor had killed Trenton. She was at the location and began to give a description of the murder scene, which was odd, because I didn't ask her for the gory details. The conversation was awkward. In my opinion, she didn't sound surprised nor angry. I can't go back and change how I found out, but the tone of the delivery was cold and callous. That alone was sad for me. I was in disbelief for starters, moreover in shock. I gathered my things quickly and whispered to another manager my son had been shot. I then went to my vehicle and my body had a slight tremble. I was unable to crank my car in the moment. I sat there with deep sadness as tears rolled down my face and begin to pray, "Lord help me, help my son!"

I left the job in route to my apartment. Soon as I entered the door, I received another phone call that a Caucasian female was shot during the shooting, and she was fighting for her life. At the time, I was given limited information about her condition. As I was planning to travel, my older son called in a rage. I couldn't get him to calm down. He was upset and stated the police were looking for him. My intention was to make it to him before they found him, but my parole officer stated they needed 48 hours to approve my travel pass. This gave me more time to process what had happened and prepare myself for the journey ahead. I decided not to take any more phone calls that day. I just needed to collect myself. The last call I took was from the adopted son. He offered his sympathy and stated he believes he was the last person who spoke with Trenton before he was murdered.

The following day, April 30, 2019, my surviving son was apprehended for first-degree murder and attempted second-degree murder. Two weeks later, the adopted son was arrested for accessory after the fact to the same charges, accused of helping Trevor dispose of potential evidence. Coroners stated in their report, both victims were shot multiple times close-range, with my son being shot the most and added he was also run over by the truck of the driver who shot him. It was described as overkill and a crime of passion.

CHAPTER 40:
KILLING ME SOFTLY

Here I was, losing my children all over again, one to death, and one to prison with eight grandchildren in total devastation. This tragedy affected us all in different ways, yet the same. These children lost a father or uncle to death or prison. And now one twin must live the rest of his life without the other. I remember the funeral like it was yesterday. The adopted family oversaw the burial. The preacher they chose talked about me as if I wasn't there. I sat there humiliated in silence. He stated that the adopted family found my children in an abandoned house, which was far from the truth, and analyzed his words to suggest my boy's vindictive behavior started with the biological mother and not the adopted family. Not sure why he felt the need to place blame or set the record straight, but the sermon was certainly inappropriate. A few people walked out in dismay before he could finish. Despite this, I kept my composure and relied on those who were there to support me. Seeing my classmates made all the difference in the world and my family stood by me.

I've experienced grief multiple times. Throughout my teenage years and adulthood, I lost my great-grandmother, grandmother and mother to death, but the loss of my sons in this way was rare. I had never dealt with anything like this before or similar to it. At the time, I was more concerned about my grandchildren and how it affected them. I shifted my focus to their welfare and well-being and sought out ways to support them. I was in contact with their moms more than usual and attentive to their care. I realized we all needed time to heal and recover. This traumatic event was a major crisis that would affect our family for generations to come. What began to stir in my heart over time was, "How could we help others who suffered distress in this manner or if our story could prevent this from happening to another family." Today, a few of us are sharing our testimonials at speaking engagements and participating in rallies that support putting an end to gun violence. We encourage counseling and medical supervision to those who suffer from substance abuse use, grief, child-abandonment issues, anxiety or depression.

CHAPTER 41:
WE CAN MAKE IT

Toward the end of the year, November 23, 2019, the baby of my deceased son was born. He was the first grandchild I was able to meet while being sober. I was either active in my addiction or incarcerated with the others. I was eight and a half years clean at the time. My oldest grandchild was 9, which is now 13, and one of the authors of this book. In other words, most of my grandchildren were born while I was in prison. His birth gave me balance. The joy of having him didn't remove the pain of losing my son, but it gave me new strength that continues to carry me even now. I compliment his mom at this time because she made sure we stayed connected. To her, I say "Thank you." She may not know this, but more often than not, the photos and videos she would send of Baby Trent brought me through some difficult times. She still does it to this very day. I must say, we all have pulled together as a family unit showing continued love and support.

CHAPTER 42:
LIFE LESSONS

January 13, 2020, I was approaching my final semester. I graduated with honors and successfully completed my Certification in Human Services Technology at Houston Community College. I was certified to practice counseling under a licensed professional. I sought out employment at a methadone clinic nearby my first job and was hired immediately. I continued my education as I worked both jobs. By the summer of 2021, I had a second graduation obtaining my associate degree and paving the way to become licensed to practice Chemical Dependency Counseling in the state of Texas. After completing 4000 clinical hours and passing the exam, I was fully licensed. Here I was again setting goals and achieving them despite the obstacles. The victories kept me balanced and gave me the stamina I needed to press my way through.

Through my setbacks, failures and accomplishments, the most endearing component was God. He positioned Himself over my life and contended with those things I could not see. Only a Sovereign God could save me. There was a time I knew of Him, I heard of Him, but I didn't know Him if that makes sense. I was oblivious to the fact that prayer was about communicating with God. My whole life, I thought it was a cry for help. As a little girl in church, I would hear the hymns and, in my mind, the sound created a moan for help in times of trouble. So, I would always pray when I was in a bad situation. No one taught me any different. My time in prison is when I formed a relationship with God. That's where I learned how to depend on Him for my everyday living instead of in times of distress. He "became" the center of my life. Meaning I discovered this analogy later in my development. I did not know He could show me how to live. In my opinion, this was the true beginning of my transformation.

As I travel back in time and study past events of my existence, I can see where near-death experiences are what gave me the desire to live. I was fighting for my life and didn't even know it. Every form of abuse that was used against me as a child throughout my teenage years to adulthood has been transformed into empowerment. I now have the will to live and compassion for those who do not. I have learned this journey was more about building my ability to help someone else.

CHAPTER 43:
AT THE END OF THE RAINBOW

In the year 2020, my interest grew in buying a house. I had dreams of being a homeowner all along. I wanted a bigger place concerning the vision God gave me for a family-size home. My apartment was small, close to efficiency size and I knew it was a steppingstone to greater. Nevertheless, I treated it with love and designed it beautifully. During my first few months in Houston, while living in the shelter, I took a First-time Home Buyer Education Class, which taught me about money management, budgeting and creditworthiness. I had no credit, so in my case, it took 3 years to get it established. By this time, I was fully prepared. My next step was finding a Realtor. To her, I say thank you. She then lead me to a program in the city of Houston that was helping qualified citizens purchase homes, providing a percentage of the down payment. A year later, on April 13, 2021, I was awarded $150,000 by the city of Houston to purchase my own residence. On June 1, 2021, I was moving into a $230,000 two-story home, perfect and spacious for a family. I am still grateful and thankful to Community Land Trust for such great assistance.

ACKNOWLEDGEMENT & DEDICATION

To the God Who snatched me out of the realm of darkness into His Marvelous light, thank you for keeping me close to Your heart and not losing sight of me when I lost my way.

To my mother, Valerie Denise Demery, thank you for the strengths and weaknesses you passed down to me. When I think of you, my faith leaps and I take the risk to accomplish goals I would have never achieved without your impartation. At a young tender age, you carried me and brought me into this world. To my surviving children, Trevor Marcel Williams, and Whitney Mycal Williams, I love each of you. I cannot go back and retrieve time and give you all a different upbringing, but I can pray, live by example and share what God has given me with both of you. To Trenton Markel Williams, my son that passed away, I love you and I miss you. The discomfort of your departure has not faded away; somehow the pain of losing you has transformed into a passion to encourage families and siblings who have suffered the same loss. I could not have written this book without you. You have ignited a fire and left a legacy that will send a message of healing to families around the nation. To my grandchildren, I could not love you all enough. I am thanking each of you for the unconditional love you all gave me soon after my incarceration. You all gravitated towards me and kept me rooted in love and grounded in faith. To my family, I find treasures in each of you. I love you all.

I end this book by saying, dear reader, I am grateful and honored to have shared my story with you. Thank you for your support.

www.ingramcontent.com/pod-product-compliance
Lightning Source LLC
Chambersburg PA
CBHW051214120626
46547CB00013B/1349